Contents

Marley's Ghost

The cellar-door flew open with a booming sound, and then he heard the noise much louder, on the floors below; then coming up the stairs, then coming straight towards his door.

'It's humbug, still!' said Scrooge. 'I won't believe it.'

His colour changed though when, without a pause, it came on through the heavy door, and passed into the room before his eyes. Upon coming in, the dying flame leaped up, as though it cried, 'I know him! Marley's ghost!' and fell again.

The same face: the very same. Marley in his pigtail, usual waistcoat, tights, and boots … The chain he drew was clasped about his middle. It was long and wound about him like a tail. It was made of cash-boxes, keys, padlocks, **ledgers**, deeds and heavy purses wrought in steel. His body was transparent, so that Scrooge observing him, and looking through his waistcoat, could see the two buttons on his coat behind …

Nor did he believe it even now. Though he looked the **phantom** through and through and saw it standing before him. Though he felt the chilling influence of his death-cold eyes … he was still **incredulous**, and fought against his senses.

'How now!' said Scrooge, **caustic** and cold as ever. 'What do you want with me?'

'Much!' – Marley's voice, no doubt about it.

'Who are you?'

'Ask me who I *was*.'

'Who *were* you then?' said Scrooge, raising his voice …

'In life I was your partner, Jacob Marley … You don't believe in me,' observed the Ghost.

'I don't,' said Scrooge …

At this the spirit raised a frightful cry, and shook its chain with such a dismal and appalling noise, that Scrooge held on tight to his chair to save himself from falling in a **swoon**. But how much greater was his

Nelson Comprehension

Pupil Book

4

Wendy Wren
Series Editor: John Jackman

OXFORD
UNIVERSITY PRESS

Great Clarendon Street, Oxford, OX2 6DP, United Kingdom

Oxford University Press is a department of the University of Oxford.
It furthers the University's objective of excellence in research, scholarship,
and education by publishing worldwide. Oxford is a registered trade mark of
Oxford University Press in the UK and in certain other countries

First published by Nelson Thornes Ltd in 2009
This edition published by Oxford University Press in 2014

British Library Cataloguing in Publication Data
Data available

978-1-4085-0549-6

7

Printed in China

Acknowledgements

Cover: Studio Pulsar at Beehive Illustration
Illustrations: Paul Moran, Pete Smith, Studio Pulsar, Studio Bugs, Gary Joynes, Bob Moulder,
Mark Draisey, Roger Penwill, Russ Daff, Tony Forbes, Melanie Sharp, Mike Phillips and David
Russell Illustration
Photographs: Alamy 10, 11, 14, 47, 49 (axe), 49 (crown), 50 (Countess of Salisbury), 62, 63;
Getty Images 42, 43, 44, 45, 49 (gate), 60, 61; iStock 20, 21, 28, 46, 50 (Anne Boleyn); NASA 12,
13; National Library of Australia 40, 41
Page make-up: Topics – The Creative Partnership, Exeter

The author and publisher are grateful to the following for permission to reproduce copyright
material:

Andersen Press Ltd for material from Melvin Burgess, *The Earth Giant* (1995) pp. 13-15; Clare
Bevan for her poem, 'Coral Reef'; Egmont Books for material from Michael Morpurgo, *Why
the Whales Came* (1985) pp. 80-82; Express Newspapers for Penny Stretton, 'The Northern
Lights Fantastic', *Daily Express*, 20.12.08; David Higham Associates on behalf of the author for
material from Michael Morpurgo, *The Ghost of Grania O'Malley*, Egmont (1996) pp. 81-82; and
Michael Morpurgo, *Kensuke's Kingdom*, Egmont (1999) pp. 42-46; Julie Holder for her poem, 'The
Loner'; Patricia Leighton for her poem, 'Bullied'; Patrick Nobes for material from his edition
of *Frankenstein*, Hutchinson Education (1984) pp. 17-19; The Random House Group Ltd for
material from Joe Simpson, *Touching the Void*, Jonathan Cape (2004) pp.71-73; Rogers Coleridge
& White Ltd on behalf of the author for Brian Patten, 'The River's Story' from *Thawing Frozen
Frogs* by Brian Patten, Viking Children's Books (1990). Copyright © Brian Patten 1990; and Jane
Serraillier on behalf of the Estate of the author for material from Ian Serraillier, *The Enchanted
Island*, Oxford University Press (1964) pp. 111-113. Copyright © 1964 Estate of Ian Serraillier.

horror when, the phantom, taking off the bandage round his head as if it were too warm to wear indoors, its lower jaw dropped down upon its breast.

Scrooge fell upon his knees and clasped his hands before his face.

'Mercy!' he said. 'Dreadful **apparition**, why do you trouble me?'

'Man of the worldly mind!' replied the Ghost, 'do you believe in me or not?'

'I do,' said Scrooge. 'I must. But why do spirits walk the earth, and why do they come to me?'

'It is required of every man,' the Ghost returned, 'that the spirit within him should walk abroad among his fellow-men, and travel far and wide, and if that spirit goes not forth in life, it is condemned to do so after death. It is doomed to wander through the world – oh, woe is me – and witness what it cannot share, but might have shared on earth, and turned to happiness!' …

'But you were always a good man of business, Jacob,' faltered Scrooge …

'Business!' cried the Ghost, wringing his hands. 'Mankind was my business; the common welfare was my business; charity, mercy, **forbearance** … Hear me! My time is nearly gone.'

'I will,' said Scrooge, 'but don't be hard on me!' …

'I am here tonight to warn you, that you have yet a chance and hope of escaping my fate … You will be haunted by Three Spirits.'

'Is that that chance and hope you mentioned, Jacob?' Scrooge demanded in a faltering voice.

'It is.'

'I – I think I'd rather not,' said Scrooge.

'Without their visits,' said the Ghost, 'you cannot hope to **shun** the path I tread. Expect the first tomorrow, when the bell tolls one.'

A Christmas Carol, Charles Dickens

- What is the name of the Ghost?
- Who is he haunting?
- Why did the Ghost make 'a frightful cry' and shake his chain?
- What did the Ghost tell Scrooge to expect tomorrow?
- Explain the meaning of the words in **bold**.
- How does Scrooge feel about the Ghost:
  - when it first appears
  - at the end of the extract?
- Why do you think the Ghost has to drag the chain around with him?
- What do you think the Ghost means when he says, 'It is required of every man that the spirit within him should walk abroad among his fellow-men'?
- What do you think Scrooge means when he says that Jacob was 'a good man of business'?
- In your own words, explain why you think Scrooge is being haunted.

Hamlet, Prince of Denmark

The King has died suddenly and mysteriously. The Queen has married her dead husband's brother who has now become King. Prince Hamlet is very unhappy about his father's death and his mother's remarriage.

One bitterly cold winter night, on the wind-swept battlements of the royal castle at Elsinore the sentries were changing guard. Except for their shouts as they challenged each other and the muffled thunder of the sea on the rocks below, all was quiet; not a mouse was stirring.

Suddenly the sound of footsteps briskly marching …

'Halt! Who goes there?' cried Bernardo, the relief officer, as a figure rose up in front of him. He was so nervous that he had forgotten to wait to be challenged first.

'No, *you* answer *me*! Give me the password,' came the answer.

'"Long live the King."'

'Are you Bernardo?'

'Yes.'

'You're very punctual.'

'It's past midnight, Francisco. Get to bed. Horatio and Marcellus are sharing the watch with me. If you see them, tell them to hurry.'

'I can hear them coming – here they are,' said Francisco. And when he had challenged and greeted the two newcomers, he lowered his pike. Wishing them good night, he marched off down the rocky path to the barracks, relieved that his freezing watch was over and quite unaware that anything unusual had happened to disturb Bernardo.

'Has this ghost appeared again?' said Horatio, half jokingly.

'I have seen nothing,' said Bernardo.

'Horatio thinks we have only imagined it,' said Marcellus. 'He won't believe we have both seen it twice. That's why I have asked him to share our watch tonight in case it appears again.'

'Nonsense. I'm sure it won't appear,' said Horatio, who was too matter-of-fact and level-headed to be superstitious.

Understanding the extract

- What is the setting for the extract?
- Who are the characters?
- What unusual thing have two of the soldiers seen?
- What happened when Horatio 'tried to question it'?
- When they left the battlements, what were the three soldiers going to do?

Looking at words

Explain the meaning of these words as they are used in the extract.

a battlements	**b** punctual	**c** pike
d level-headed	**e** superstitious	**f** majestic
g haggard	**h** harrowed	**i** dumb

'Last night, at the stroke of one –' Bernardo began, then broke off abruptly.

A tall majestic figure had loomed out of the darkness and stood before them, shimmering in the moonlight. Armed from head to foot, the helmet visor raised, it had a pale and haggard face and grizzled beard and seemed to be floating in the air.

'It's like our dead King,' Bernardo gasped.

'Exactly like him,' agreed Horatio, harrowed with fear and wonder.

He steadied his nerves and strode boldly forward. Holding his sword in front of him hilt upwards like a cross, he tried to question it. But it stalked away into the shadows as if it had been offended.

What could this vision mean? Clad in the same armour he had worn in the Norwegian war, it was the very image of the dead King. Why had he returned to haunt them? Could it be because the Norwegians, defeated in the recent war, were threatening to attack again and recover the land they had lost? As they paced up and down, Horatio and the two officers anxiously discussed these questions but could find no answer.

Suddenly, when the night was almost over, the ghost appeared again. Horatio stood in its path and challenged it. It seemed about to speak some message, when in the distance a cock crowed. Then it turned its head and began to drift away.

They cried out; they tried to trap it, to strike it with their pikes, but it melted into the shadows and all they struck was empty air.

Already the first gleams of dawn had splashed the eastern hills. Their watch over, the three soldiers left the battlements and returned to the palace, determined to tell Hamlet what they had seen. Hamlet was the dead King's son. Perhaps the ghost, who had been dumb to them, would speak to him.

The Enchanted Island, Ian Serraillier

Exploring further

- Why do you think the ghostly scene is set 'One bitterly cold winter night'?
- What impression do you get of Horatio?
- Why do you think that Horatio held his sword up 'like a cross'?
- Why do you think the ghost 'began to drift away' when 'a cock crowed'?
- Why do you think the ghost keeps appearing on the battlements?

 Extra

Make the extract into a playscript and prepare it for performance.
Remember, you will need:

The scene; the characters; dialogue; stage directions that 'tell the story'; stage directions that tell the actors how to speak and what to do.

The Ghostly Girl

Mandy awoke suddenly in the night, trembling with fear. Moonlight flooded her bedroom with silver and shadow. It was only a dream, she told herself, only a dream. So why was she shivering in a warm bed?

A memory of the dream returned and she threw back the bedclothes and switched on the light. It had all seemed so real, and she'd never had a fright like that before.

She wrapped a dressing-gown around her and opened the door. The house was quiet, the passage in darkness, as she felt her way along the wall to her brother's room. She opened the door and closed it behind her, switched on the light.

Joe's room was full of aeroplane models, and she had to move carefully to avoid them. She sat on the edge of his bed and shook him hard; Joe was a heavy sleeper.

Presently, her brother stirred. 'What's up, then? Mandy …'

'I had a nightmare, Joe. It scared me – I've got to talk to somebody.'

Joe was twelve, two years younger than his sister, and sturdy, with unruly fair hair. Mandy shuddered. 'It was horrid!'

Joe sat up reluctantly; he was still sleepy. 'What was it about?'

'I was walking along, through a mist, and all round me were ruins. It was nowhere I've ever seen, I'm sure of that. And then *she* came towards me, through the mist. Her feet didn't touch the ground – she just drifted along. I could see right through her, Joe. She was a ghost, a girl of about my age in a long dress, and with a pale face. Her mouth was moving as if she was trying to say something, but I couldn't hear what it was – like watching the old silent movies on telly. That's all, really, because I woke up. But it was so real.' She forced a laugh. 'I don't know why I was scared so much – it was only a dream.'

Joe rubbed sleep from his eyes and looked hard at his sister. 'You do look a bit white … Still, I never heard of anyone dreaming a ghost before.' He sounded impressed.

Mandy stood up. 'I'll be all right now, Joe. Thanks for listening.'

She tiptoed back to her room, and it was a long time before she fell asleep.

A week later, Mandy dreamed again. She stood among the ruins of an old house and it was dark. The ghost girl appeared before her, rippling as if seen through water. She felt icy cold. The ghost drifted nearer and lifted an arm, reaching out a hand to touch her …

Mandy awoke abruptly, soaked with sweat, her heart thumping wildly. She pushed bedclothes into her mouth to stop herself screaming. It was ridiculous, she thought, scared silly by a dream …

At the breakfast table, her mother commented, 'You look off-colour, Mandy. Are you sleeping all right?'

Joe hastily swallowed a spoonful of cereal. 'Was it the dream again?'

Their father looked up from his newspaper crossword. 'What dream's this? First I've heard of it.'

'She dreamed a ghost,' Joe said proudly.

Dream Ghost, Sydney J Bounds

Understanding the extract
1 When did Mandy have the first dream?
2 Who did she go to talk to after the first dream?
3 What did the girl in the dream look like?
4 At what point did Mandy wake up:
   a in the first dream   **b** in the second dream?

Understanding the words
5 Explain the meaning of these words and phrases as they are used in the extract.
   a avoid   **b** nightmare   **c** unruly
   d reluctantly   **e** silent movies   **f** ridiculous

Exploring further
6 Find evidence in the extract to show how Mandy reacted to the first dream.
7 Why do you think Mandy told her brother about her dream but not her parents?
8 What impression do you get of Mandy?
9 How do you think Mandy's parents will react now that they know about the dreams?
10 Do you think Mandy was more or less frightened the second time she had the dream? Explain your reasons.

Extra
Think of as many reasons as you can for why Mandy is having this dream. Choose the one you think is most likely.

Emmeline Pankhurst

Emmeline Goulden was born in Manchester in 1858. Her father was a **self-made man** who had begun his working life as an office boy and risen to be a successful businessman. Emmeline grew up in a typical Victorian household where the father was master.

When Emmeline was fourteen, she was sent to Paris for her education. On her return, she married Richard Pankhurst who was a **barrister**. In the following years she had four children: Christabel, Sylvia, Frank and Ada. Emmeline had been a dutiful daughter; it now seemed as if she had settled into being a **dutiful** wife and mother.

Her husband, however, was not like her father. He had very different ideas about the role of women and encouraged Emmeline to see herself as his equal. She soon realised, however, that although she was an equal to her husband at home, outside she was just like other women – **a second-class citizen**. Women could not vote or become Members of Parliament so they had no power to change anything.

Emmeline, with a group of **like-minded** women, formed the WSPU (Women's Social and Political Union) and began to demand that women had the vote. The main political parties showed little interest in giving women the right to vote, despite massive demonstrations outside the Houses of Parliament. At this point, Emmeline decided there would be a change of **tactics**.

Members of the WSPU smashed windows, burned postboxes and set fire to unoccupied buildings. Some of the women were arrested and sent to jail. Emmeline was jailed for the first time in 1908. Women prisoners began hunger strikes and were brutally force-fed. When their health was in danger they were released, only to be re-arrested when their health improved.

This state of affairs continued until the beginning of the First World War. With the men away fighting, women turned their attention to keeping the country going: working in factories and on farms, driving ambulances, and generally doing all the work that their absent fathers, husbands and sons could not.

By the end of the war, it was generally accepted that women should have a right to vote. Women over the age of 30 were given the vote in 1918, but it was not until 1928, the year of Emmeline's death, that all women were given the vote on the same terms as men.

- Where and when was Emmeline born?
- Where did she go for her education?
- Who did she marry?
- What organisation did she form?
- What did the organisation want?
- Explain the meaning of the words and phrases in **bold**.
- Explain, in your own words, the meaning of the phrase 'father was master'.
- In what way was Emmeline's husband's attitude to women different from her father's?
- Why do you think it was 'generally accepted that women should have a right to vote' at the end of the First World War?
- There are seven paragraphs in the biography. Say briefly what each one is about.
- How is the biography organised?
- Why do you think the writer has included photographs?

Neil Armstrong

Neil Alden Armstrong was born on 5 August 1930 in Wapakoneta, Ohio, in the United States. His father worked for the Ohio government and the family moved around the state, and lived in twenty different towns. He was fascinated by aeroplanes from a very early age and was determined to get his pilot's licence.

In 1947, after leaving Blume High School, Neil went to Purdue University to study aerospace engineering on a navy scholarship. In 1949, he was called up to serve in the navy, and eighteen months later he was a qualified naval aviator. He served as a navy pilot in the Korean War and flew 78 combat missions.

Back in America, he completed his science degree in 1955. He then worked for NASA (National Aeronautics and Space Administration) from 1955 to 1971. During the following years he worked as an engineer and test pilot. He flew 200 different types of aircraft, including jets, rockets, helicopters and gliders.

He applied, and was accepted, for astronaut training in 1962. Three years later, in 1965, he was the Command Pilot for *Gemini 8*. It was launched on 16 March 1966. The purpose of the mission was to dock with an unmanned craft, *Agena*, in space, and it was successfully accomplished.

Understanding the biography
- Where and when was Neil Armstrong born?
- What did he serve as in the Korean War?
- When he had completed his science degree, what job did he do?
- What happened in:

  a 1962   b 1966   c 1969?

Looking at words
Explain the meaning of these words and phrases as they are used in the biography.

a fascinated by   b scholarship   c aviator

d unmanned   e accomplished

On 23 December 1968, Armstrong was chosen as the Commander for *Apollo 11*, the manned mission to the moon.

Apollo 11 was to orbit the moon, and the lunar module, called Eagle, was to land on the surface. Along with Armstrong, Buzz Aldrin and Mike Collins made up the crew. Mike Collins would remain in Apollo 11 while Armstrong and Aldrin landed on the moon in Eagle.

On 16 July 1969, *Apollo 11* was launched from the Kennedy Space Centre in Florida. On 20 July, Eagle touched down on the moon's surface. Neil Armstrong was the first man to walk on the moon and, as he stepped out of the lunar module, he said, 'That's one small step for man, one giant leap for mankind.'

Armstrong and Aldrin spent a total of 21 hours and 36 minutes on the moon collecting samples of rock and dust. *Apollo 11* returned to Earth, 8 days, 3 hours and 18 minutes after take-off.

Armstrong worked at NASA until, in 1971, he became Professor of Aerospace Engineering at the University of Cincinnati. He has received many honours for his historic moon landing, including the Presidential Medal of Freedom and the NASA Distinguished Service Medal.

Exploring further
- What three pieces of evidence in the biography tell you that Armstrong was interested in flying?
- Explain, in your own words, what *Gemini 8's* mission was.
- Why do you think the astronauts collected samples of moon rock and dust?
- Explain, in your own words, what you think Armstrong meant when he said, 'That's one small step for man, one giant leap for mankind.'
- There are eight paragraphs in the biography. Explain briefly what each one is about.
- How is the biography organised?

Extra
Space travel is very expensive. It has cost America millions of dollars. Do you think money should be spent in this way or not? Explain your reasons.

Louis Braille

Louis Braille was born in 1809, in the small town of Coupray, near Paris. His father made harnesses and other leather goods, and one of the tools he used was an awl. This is a short pointed stick used to punch holes into leather.

Louis liked to watch his father at work in his workshop. When he was three years old, he was playing with an awl when his hand slipped and he injured himself in the eye. At first, the wound did not seem too serious, but it became infected and within a few days Louis was blind in both eyes.

In the years that followed, he attended the local school. He was a very bright pupil, but learning was difficult because he could not read or write; he could only listen.

At the age of ten he was sent to the Royal Institute for Blind Youth in Paris. Here, Louis learned to read from books with raised letters, but the system was not very successful as it was difficult to tell the letters apart. Also, the books were bulky and expensive. The school only had fourteen of them. Louis read all of the fourteen books but it took a long time to work out the letters, then the words, and then the sentences. He was sure there must be a way to make 'reading' with his fingers quicker and easier.

One day, a soldier called Charles Barbier visited the school. He had invented a system called 'night writing' that allowed messages from officers to be read by soldiers in the dark. The system consisted of raised dots and dashes. The soldiers had to learn what the dots and dashes represented, then they could run their fingers over them to 'read' the message.

Louis tried the code and, although it was much better than the bulky books, it was still very slow. The dashes took up a lot of space so very little could be written on each page. Louis spent a great deal of time trying to improve the 'night writing'. He wanted to make it less complicated and to get more words on a page.

In the school vacation he worked on the problem. The solution came to him by handling the very tool that had made him blind. He could use a blunt awl to make a raised dot alphabet. It consisted of up to six dots, arranged in different positions, to represent the letters of the alphabet.

He published his first Braille book in 1829 and by 1837 had added symbols for music and maths. His system, surprisingly, was not greeted with great enthusiasm, and it took many years before it was universally accepted.

a	b	c	d	e	f	g	h	i	j	k	l	m

n	o	p	q	r	s	t	u	v	w	x	y	z

Understanding the biography

1 Where and when was Louis Braille born?

2 What did his father do?

3 What happened to Louis when:

   a he was three years old   **b** he was ten years old

   c he was twenty years old?

Understanding the words

4 Explain the meaning of these words and phrases as they are used in the biography.

   a harnesses   **b** infected   **c** bulky   **d** consisted of
   e less complicated   **f** symbols   **g** universally accepted

Exploring further

5 In what ways do you think only being able to listen to your teacher and not being able to read and write notes would be difficult?

6 Explain, in your own words, how 'night writing' worked.

7 What impression do you get of Louis Braille from this biography?

8 There are eight paragraphs in the biography. Write briefly what each one is about.

9 How is the biography organised?

Extra

Using the illustration of the Braille alphabet, write your own name in Braille.

15

The Brook

I come from **haunts** of coot and hern,
  I make a sudden **sally**,
And sparkle out among the fern,
  To bicker down a valley.

By thirty hills I hurry down,
  Or slip between the ridges,
By twenty **thorps**, a little town,
  And half a hundred bridges.

I chatter over stony ways,
  In little sharps and trebles,
I bubble into eddying bays,
  I babble on the pebbles.

With many a curve my banks I **fret**
  By many a field and fallow,
Any many a fairy **foreland** set
  With willow-weed and mallow.

I chatter, chatter, as I flow
  To join the brimming river,
For men may come and men may go,
  But I go on for ever.

I wind about, and in and out,
    With here a blossom sailing,
And here and there a **lusty** trout,
    And here and there a grayling.

And here and there a foamy flake
    Upon me, as I travel
With many a silvery waterbreak
    Above the golden gravel,

And draw them all along, and flow
    To join the brimming river,
For men may come and men may go,
    But I go on for ever.

I slip, I slide, I gloom, I glance,
    Among my skimming swallows;
I make the netted sunbeam dance
    Against my sandy shallows.

I murmur under moon and stars
    In brambly wildernesses;
I linger by my shingly bars;
    I **loiter** round my cresses;

And out again I curve and flow
    To join the brimming river,
For men may come and men may go,
    But I go on for ever.

'*The Brook*', Alfred Lord Tennyson

, Where does the brook come from?

, Where is it going to?

, When is the brook moving:
• quickly
• slowly?

, Explain the meaning of the words and phrases in **bold**.

, What human qualities is the brook given in this poem?

, If the brook was human, what sort of person do you think it would be?

, Why do you think the poet has used the sound words 'chatter', 'babble' and 'murmur'?

, Explain the meaning of the last two lines of the poem in your own words.

, Explain why you like, or do not like, the poem.

The River's Story

I remember when life was good.
I shilly-shallied across meadows,
Tumbled down mountains,
I laughed and gurgled through woods,
Stretched and yawned in a myriad of floods.
Insects, weightless as sunbeams,
Settled upon my skin to drink.
I wore lily-pads like medals.
Fish, lazy and battle-scarred,
Gossiped beneath them.
The damselflies were my ballerinas,
The pike my ambassadors.
Kingfishers, disguised as rainbows,
Were my secret agents.
It was a sweet-time, a gone-time,
A time before factories grew,
Brick by greedy brick,
And left me cowering
In monstrous shadows.
Like drunken giants
They vomited their poison into me.
Tonight a scattering of vagrant bluebells,
Dwarfed by the same poisons,
Toll my ending.

Understanding the poem

- Where did the river flow 'when life was good'?
- Name three groups of living things associated with the river.
- What has happened around the river that has changed everything?
- What is now left of the river?

Looking at words

Explain the meaning of these words and phrases as they are used in the poem.

a myriad   b ambassadors   c cowering

d vomited   e vagrant   f Toll my ending

g I am your inheritance   h derelict   i remnants

Children, come and find me if you wish,
I am your inheritance.
Behind the derelict housing-estates
You will discover my remnants.
Clogged with garbage and junk
To an open sewer I've shrunk,
I, who have flowed through history,
Who have seen hamlets become villages,
Villages become towns, towns become cities,
Am reduced to a trickle of filth
Beneath the still burning stars.

'The River Pattern', Brian Patten

Exploring further
- Why do you think the poet has made the river human?
- If the river was human, how do you think it felt when:
    a 'life was good'   **b** 'factories grew'?
- Why do you think the fish were 'battle-scarred'?
- What does the river mean when it says it has 'flowed through history'?
- What do you think 'The River's Story' is warning us about?

Extra
Using the information in the poem, make a poster to warn people about polluting our rivers. Write the text and illustrate the poster as if it was the river speaking.

Coral Reef

I am a teeming city;
An underwater garden
Where fishes fly;
A lost forest
of skeleton trees;
A home for starry anemones;
A hiding place for frightened fishes;
A skulking place for prowling predators;
An alien world
Whose unseen monsters
Watch with luminous eyes;
An ancient palace topped by
Improbable towers;
A mermaid's maze;
A living barrier built on
Uncountable small deaths;
An endlessly growing sculpture;
A brittle mystery;
A vanishing trick;
A dazzling wonder
More magical than all
Your earthbound dreams;
I am a priceless treasure;
A precious heirloom,
And I am yours

To love
Or to lose
As you choose.

'Coral Reef', Clare Bevan

Understanding the poem

1 Find three things normally found on land that the coral reef says it is.

2 What do 'frightened fishes' use the coral reef for?

3 What choice do people have to make about coral reefs?

Understanding the words

4 Explain the meaning of these words as they are used in the poem.
   a teeming   **b** skeleton   **c** predators
   d luminous   **e** brittle   **f** heirloom

Exploring further

5 Explain what the poet means when she says that the coral reef is:
   a 'built on / Uncountable small deaths'
   b 'An endlessly growing sculpture'

6 What do you think the 'unseen monsters' are?

7 Why do you think the towers are described as 'improbable'?

8 The poet has given the coral reef a voice. What warning is the coral reef giving to the reader?

9 If the coral reef was human, what sort of person do you think it would be?

Extra

Using what you have learnt from the poem, write briefly about why you think we should, or should not, protect coral reefs.

Frankenstein

It was on a dark, sad night in November that I came to the end of my work. Most of what I had done had never been tried by anyone else before. It was quite impossible to get a perfect result from this first attempt. I had aimed at beauty, but the face of the creature I made was horrible. His skin was yellow, and hardly hid the muscles and **arteries** under it. His eyes were dull and the whites were almost the same colour as the yellow skin. The eyes were deep in his head. True, his hair was black and long, and his teeth were very white. But these touches of beauty only made the rest of his face appear more horrible.

His **limbs** were the right shape, but they were huge. One of the most difficult parts of the work was joining together the very tiny nerves and veins. Nobody had tried this before, and there were no scientific tools with which to do it. I had to work to a larger scale than normal, and I decided to make my creature eight feet high.

I looked down at this ugly thing, and wondered whether all my hard work had been worth it. I had driven myself on, and was ill as a result. Often I had almost given up the work, when I failed to do some particularly difficult part of it. But always I had started again. And here was the result of a year's work.

I felt certain that I could now bring my **creation** to life. The body was linked up with the wires and switches that would make use of electrical power to give it life.

As I looked at the ugly creation, I almost decided to destroy it and forget the whole idea. I wish I had. But I was not strong enough to turn away from the dream of being the creator of a race of beings who would serve me as their master. I wanted to use my great scientific powers to become a sort of god.

So I decided to carry on. A storm was building up over the city. I watched it and waited. Suddenly at about one in the morning, **the storm broke**. Within moments my mast was doing its work, and feeding down the power that I needed to put the spark of life into my creation. I watched, and moved the controls of my machines. Would it all work?

For some time nothing happened, and I began to wonder whether all my work had been **in vain**.

And then I saw the yellow eyes of the creature open. They moved from side to side. Then its chest began to move up and down and I could hear the sound of breathing. Soon the control board showed the steady beating of the heart. I fed in more power through the limbs, and the arms and legs began to jerk into life.

The creature began to move, and slowly sat up. I realized that it was even more horrible in life than it had been lying there with no life in it. My dream had been one of beauty, and instead I had created an ugly monster. My only wish was to escape from it, and I had no other thought in my mind. I ran out of the laboratory, and slammed the door behind me. I was full of **disgust** at what I had done.

Frankenstein, adapted by Patrick Nobes from the novel by Mary Shelley

› When does this part of the story take place?

› What did the creature look like?

› Why had the narrator 'almost given up the work'?

› How did the narrator bring the creature to life?

› What did the narrator do when the creature 'slowly sat up'?

› Explain the meaning of the words and phrases in **bold**.

› Find evidence in the extract to suggest that the narrator was a scientist.

› Explain, in your own words, what the narrator's 'dream' was.

› In what way had he succeeded and failed?

› We know what the narrator feels when the creature comes to life. How do you think the creature feels?

› What do you think happens next?

The Earth Giant

One night, there is a great storm. Amy and her brother, Peter, hear a terrible noise like a dying giant, and a great oak is ripped out of the ground half a mile away. Amy is sure there is something under that tree and goes to find out what.

She moved to another spot and began again but she uncovered only stones and roots. She tried again and again. All her senses told her there was something here, but the clay was completely dead.

At last she gave up and sat unhappily in the crater. She felt like crying. It was all wrong!

Then, slowly into her mind came a cold, vast presence: the huge ball of clay and roots the tree had torn from the ground. She turned her head to look up at it. It towered above her into the sky. It was difficult to think such a huge object had been underground all the time; it seemed somehow vaster than the ground. And then Amy realised. What she was looking for – what had called her – wasn't underground anymore. It was where it had always been – held in the embrace of the roots of the old oak. Only now it was high up over her head …

Amy scrambled up out of the hole and began to toil up the cliff face of roots, clay and stones. She wasn't good at climbing but she was confident now. She knew where to go. She found a great broken root sticking out and sat on that, and she began to scrape.

The clay fell away in sticky clumps at first, but after the first layer it got harder. The earth and stones were packed so tightly together. She would have liked to dig with a stick, but she didn't dare. She might hurt something. Then she began to panic that Peter might come back and see and she began to shovel with both her hands as fast as she could, breaking her nails and tearing her skin. At last, she found what she was looking for.

It was almost the same colour as the earth, a deep reddish colour. It was smooth and shiny and only slightly warmer than the earth. Amy brushed it with her hand. It was round and firm. No one else would have recognised it, but Amy knew. It was part of an arm.

Understanding the extract
- What had ripped the oak tree out of the ground?
- Amy couldn't find what she was looking for in the ground. Where was it?
- Why didn't Amy want to use a stick to dig with?
- What did Amy discover?

Looking at words
Explain the meaning of these words as they are used in the extract.

a crater **b** embrace **c** toil
d confident **e** recognised **f** revealing

She moved a little further up the cliff of broken roots and began again. She dug the clay and stones away in handfuls, revealing the skin closer towards the neck. There was a pattern on it, where gravel and little stones had pressed into it over the years. A few more handfuls and the neck and the strong curve towards the shoulder came into view. Then, pressed firmly in the earth, the edge of an ear.

Amy stared. It had been a dream but it was real. She touched the skin on the ear gently with her finger. The skin was cold but Amy also knew it was not dead. It was the cold of someone, a woman or girl, who had been asleep for a long, long time – since before the old oak tree was an acorn. She had been asleep for hundreds or thousands of years, and now she was awakening again. There was no movement; the sleeper lay as still as the stones around her. Amy slowly stroked her neck and began to imagine it was getting warmer. It was only the heat of her own hand. Now she began to realise that everything was so big – the shoulder so long and high, the arm so broad. She was almost twice as big as a grown-up.

It was a giant in the earth.

The Earth Giant, Melvin Burgess

Exploring further

- Find evidence in the extract that suggests how Amy knew that 'something' was buried under the oak tree.
- How had the crater been made?
- Why do you think Amy began to 'imagine' it was getting warmer?
- How do you think Amy felt when she discovered the earth giant?
- What do you think happened next?

Extra

If you could talk to the earth giant, what questions would you ask?

Jurassic Park

John Hammond has recreated the world of dinosaurs on a remote island. These dinosaurs are not models – they are the real thing! He keeps them behind electric fences. He invites Dr Alan Grant to come and see them. John Hammond sends his grandchildren, Tim and Lex, and Dr Grant on a tour of the island in electric cars. Dr Grant and Ian are in one car, and Tim, Lex and Gennaro are in another. Suddenly the power fails, just as they are outside the Tyrannosaurus paddock!

'Did you feel that?' Tim asked. At first Lex didn't know what he was talking about. But then she felt it, too. The car was shaking.

There were loud quaking sounds and it seemed as though the earth was moving – like something was taking giant footsteps.

Gennaro's eyes widened in fear. The sound got louder. The vibrations felt stronger. Whatever it was was coming closer. And then they all saw it. Tyrannosaurus rex. It was gripping the fence. Gennaro stared in horror. Oh no, he thought. The dinosaur should have felt an electric shock. The power must be out in the fences, too! But would it break through?

The T-rex swung its mighty head. Tim gasped. Its boxy head was bigger than Tim's whole body. And its body was bigger than a bus. The dinosaur waved its short, silly-looking arms in the air. Then it clawed the fence. The Tyrannosaurus was tearing it down!

All at once Gennaro bolted out of the car. He didn't say a word. He just ran, leaving Tim and Lex all alone. Lex began to scream. But Gennaro didn't stop. He raced towards a small building a short distance down the road. Moments later, he reached it and ran inside. But the building wasn't finished yet. Gennaro couldn't lock the wooden door behind him.

'What's he doing?' Ian asked Alan. They hadn't noticed the Tyrannosaurus yet.

Then they saw the fence come down. The Tyrannosaurus was free! It stood on the park road, eyeing the two cars.

'Don't move,' Alan whispered to Ian, 'It can't see us if we don't move.'

The T-rex bent down. It peered through the car window at Ian. Ian froze. He couldn't have moved if he'd wanted to.

Suddenly the first car lit up like a beacon. Lex had turned on a flashlight. The dinosaur raised its head. It was drawn to the light.

'I'm sorry, sorry, sorry,' Lex mumbled to Tim as the T-rex thudded closer. It lifted its head high. Tim and Lex could see it through the sunroof.

Roar! The dinosaur opened its mouth wide, then roared again. It was so loud, the car windows rattled.

Then the T-rex struck.

The dinosaur lifted its powerful leg. Smash! It kicked the car. Windows shattered, and the car tilted on its side. The dinosaur lowered its head and butted the car off the road.

Inside, Tim and Lex tumbled about as the car rolled over. Now it was upside down. Tim twisted around to look out the window. They were right by the cliff.

The T-rex towered over the car. It put one leg on the frame and tore at the undercarriage of the car with its jaws. Biting at anything it could get a hold of, it ripped the rear axle free, tossed it aside, and bit a tyre. Lex and Tim were trapped. And the dinosaur was about to push them over the cliff!

Jurassic Park, adapted by Gail Herman from the novel by Michael Crichton

Understanding the extract

1 What has John Hammond done?
2 Where are the characters at the beginning of the extract?
3 Why could the T-rex grip the fence?
4 What does Gennaro do when he sees the T-rex?
5 Why does Alan say, 'Don't move'?

Understanding the words

6 Explain the meaning of these words as they are used in the extract.

a quaking	**b** vibrations	**c** bolted
d beacon	**e** butted	**f** undercarriage

Exploring further

7 How does the author create a feeling of fear in the first three paragraphs?
8 What impression do you get of Gennaro?
9 How do you know that Dr Alan Grant knows something about dinosaurs?
10 Why do you think Lex turned on the flashlight?

Extra

Imagine you are Tim or Lex. Rewrite the extract from your point of view.
Remember!

- You don't know what Alan and Ian are doing.
- You only know what is happening in your car and what you can see through the windows.
- Include your thoughts and feelings as you tell the story.

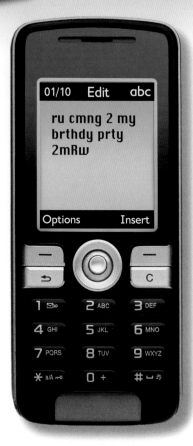

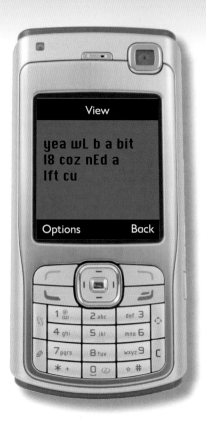

Text messaging – good or bad?

Many adults are worried about the effect text messaging is having on the standard of written English of young people today. Others think that any form of **communication** between young people should be encouraged. So what are the advantages and disadvantages of text messaging?

Firstly, text messaging is a form of communication that young people are very **enthusiastic** about. Adults should not try to stop it just because they don't understand it and probably can't do it! They should realise that text messaging is spreading into the business world, so some adults see it as a very positive thing.

Another advantage of text messaging is that it is very fast. A text can be sent and replied to in a matter of seconds, almost like speaking face to face. There is no need to log on at a computer as is the case when sending an e-mail.

Perhaps one of the most important advantages for young people is that text messaging is a very private form of communication. Unlike a conversation or telephone call that can be **overheard**, a text can be read just by the person it is sent to, unless he or she chooses to show it to others. The reply is equally private.

There are, however, serious disadvantages when it comes to the rules of text messaging creeping into written English. Parents and teachers have seen the symbols and abbreviations of text messaging in their children's school work.

Spelling is an obvious problem. It is a fact that some young children are **convinced** that text spelling is correct, for example that 'great' is always 'gr8', whether texting or writing. Vowels are usually missed out altogether.

Punctuation is another area of **concern**. As it doesn't exist in the rules of text messaging, except to form symbols – for example, :) = I'm happy – it is fast disappearing from written work. Capitals have also changed their use in texting and stand for double letters in a word, instead of the beginning of sentences and proper nouns.

Text messaging is also having an effect on children's vocabulary. Messages are written in a kind of **shorthand** so children express themselves in **stock phrases** and come to rely on a very limited vocabulary, no matter what the situation.

So what is to be done? Banning text messaging is **unrealistic** and would stop a very valuable form of communication. Allowing the rules of text messaging to go uncorrected in written work would seriously affect the standard of children's education. The answer is to teach children 'appropriate' language. Just as they understand that the way they speak to friends is different from the way they speak to their parents and teachers, so we should help them to appreciate the different rules of text messaging and standard English. Neither one is right; neither one is wrong. It is only when they are used in the wrong way that the problems occur.

> › What is the article about?
> › According to the article, what are:
>   • the advantages of text messaging
>   • the disadvantages of text messaging?
> › Explain the meaning of the words and phrases in bold.
> › What do you think is the purpose of:
>   • the first paragraph
>   • the whole article?
> › Who do you think is the intended audience?
> › What do you think is the attitude of the writer to text messaging?
> › Explain, in your own words, the conclusion the writer comes to. Do you think it is sensible or not? Explain your reasons.
> › What do you think about text messaging?

29

Animal testing

When we are ill and visit the doctor or go into hospital, we expect that the drugs we are given or the operation we have to undergo to make us better are safe. Extensive research is done on these drugs and procedures in laboratories all over the world and, for some of this work, it is necessary to use animals.

Animal testing has been essential in making such procedures as heart, lung and kidney transplants, cataract operations and joint replacements viable. This means that humans can live longer and have a better quality of life. Reducing or banning animal testing would have serious consequences for the future of medical research and the benefits it brings to us.

Many people think that animal testing is not necessary. They claim that research can be done in other ways. This is not true. Wherever possible, scientists use other methods such as computer modelling and, as a result, the number of animals used in the last 30 years has halved. However, in many cases, these non-animal methods are not suitable. The only way for some medical advances to be made is through close study of how animals react to drugs and operations.

Scientists involved in animal testing do not do so lightly, and they are constantly striving to find alternative means to make drugs and medical procedures safe for humans. They follow a code known as the 'Three Rs':

- **R**eplacement – to replace animal procedures with non-animal techniques wherever possible
- **R**eduction – to minimise the number of animals used
- **R**efinement – to improve the way experiments are carried out to make sure animals suffer as little as possible.

Understanding the article
- What is the article about?
- Explain briefly why the writer thinks animal testing is necessary.
- What has happened in the last 30 years?
- The Animals Act was passed in 1986. What does it make scientists do?

Looking at words
Explain the meaning of these words and phrases as they are used in the article.

a undergo	**b** procedures	**c** viable	**d** serious consequences
e striving	**f** minimise	**g** potential	**h** out-weighed
i effective			

The use of animals in medical research is closely regulated. In 1986, The Animal Act was passed, and scientists have to prove that the cost of the research and the potential suffering of any animal involved are far out-weighed by the likely benefits to humans. A team of inspectors, who are vets or doctors, are employed by the government to ensure that all animal testing is done to these high standards.

That animal suffering occurs is not denied. But we have to ask ourselves a simple question. If we, or our loved ones, are faced with a life-threatening condition, do we not want medical researchers to have done everything possible to make the treatment safe and effective? Yes or no?

A survey by MORI in 2002 found that 90 per cent of the public accepted the need for animal testing provided that:

- the research is for serious medical or life-saving purposes
- there is no alternative
- there is no unnecessary suffering.

So, 90 per cent of the public said 'Yes'.

Exploring further
- What is the purpose of:
  a the first paragraph   **b** the article as a whole?
- Who do you think is the intended audience?
- The writer says that the scientists involved in animal testing 'do not do so lightly'. What does this mean?
- A survey found that 90 per cent of the public agree with animal testing under certain conditions. Explain these conditions in your own words.
- Are you convinced by the writer's arguments? Why? Why not?

Extra
What arguments would you put forward to stop animal testing?

UFOs do not exist!

Strange lights in the sky! People claiming to have been abducted by aliens! *The X Files* and *Independence Day* warning us to be prepared to fight the 'baddies' from distant planets to protect our world! Well, maybe.

Let's look at the facts. These so-called unidentified flying objects are usually seen by very ordinary people, at night, and in lonely rural areas. They are almost always 'sighted' by a person on his or her own and no physical evidence is left to prove their story.

When UFOs were first 'sighted' in the 1950s, believers were convinced that Earth was being visited by Martians, Venusians, or other inhabitants of our solar system. When American and Russian space probes visited these planets and found them unable to support life, the UFO enthusiasts changed their minds and said that the 'aliens' must be from other galaxies! Their technology is so advanced they can travel faster than the speed of light to come and have a look at us.

But for what purpose? Suppose we say UFOs do exist. Suppose that we accept there are technologically superior beings who travel millions, if not billions, of light years to pay us a visit and then go away again. It doesn't make any sense. Why don't they make contact with our world leaders if they come in peace? Why don't they use their superior technology to take over our planet if they are not so peaceful? Why do they buzz around the countryside, allowing their spaceships to be seen by relatively few people, and then disappear again?

People will argue that it is not just the lone individual on a back road in the dead of night who claims to have seen strange lights in the sky, and they are right. Let's take the recent example of the 'four large glowing lights in the sky' that were reported by dozens of people from all over Wiltshire. So many people saw them, surely this is the proof we have been waiting for? Well, no. SUFOR – The Swindon UFO Research group – had to admit there was a very ordinary explanation. Cirencester College was open to the public that evening and they put on a light show that used powerful space tracer lights straight up into the sky. The light show stopped at 9.30pm and, not surprisingly, the sighting of the alien visitors stopped at the same time!

And finally – in the USA alone, five million people have claimed that they have been abducted by aliens in the last 50 years. That's 2,470 visits from UFOs every day. I wonder why I haven't seen one.

Understanding the article

1 Where and when do UFO 'sightings' usually take place?
2 When were UFOs first sighted?
3 In the fourth paragraph, what is the writer puzzled about?
4 In your own words, explain what happened recently at Cirencester College.

Understanding the words

5 Explain the meaning of these words and phrases as they are used in the article.

  a abducted   b rural   c physical evidence
  d Venusians   e space probes f superior technology

Exploring further

6 What is the purpose of:

  a the first paragraph   b the article as a whole?

7 Who do you think is the intended audience?
8 The writer repeats the fact that most UFO 'sightings' are reported by people who are alone. What is the writer implying?
9 Does the writer want the final paragraph to be taken seriously or not? Explain your reasons.
10 Are you convinced by the writer's arguments? Why? Why not?

Extra

What arguments would you put forward to say that UFOs do exist?

Unit 6

Finding a voice
(poetry dealing with issues)
▸ **Exploring issues in poetry**

The Loner

He leans against the playground wall,
Smacks his hands against the bricks
And other boredom-beating tricks,
Traces patterns with his feet,
Scuffs to make the tarmac squeak,
Back against the wall he stays –
And never plays.

The playground's **quick with life**,
The beat is strong.
Though sharp as a knife
Strife doesn't last long.
There is shouting, laughter, song,
And a place at the wall
For who won't belong.

We pass him running, skipping, walking,
In slow **huddled** groups, low talking.
Each in our familiar **clique**
We pass him by and never speak,
His loneness is his shell and shield
And neither he nor we will **yield**.

He wasn't there at the wall today,
Someone said he'd moved away
To another school and place
And on the wall where he used to lean
Someone had chalked
'Watch this space.'

'The Loner', Julie Holder

- Where and when is the poem set?
- What does the 'loner' do?
- What do the other children do?
- Where is the 'loner' at the end of the poem?
- Explain the meaning of the words and phrases in **bold**.
- Explain, in your own words, what you understand by the word 'loner'.
- What does the poet mean when she says 'And a place at the wall / For who won't belong'?
- Whose fault is it, do you think, that the loner won't play with the others?
- How do you think:
  - the loner feels about the other children
  - the other children feel about the loner?
- What do you think the poet means by the last three lines of the poem?

Bullied

Bullies get you.
I don't know how but they do.
They seem to have some
secret inborn radar
tuned in to loners,
quiet ones,
different ones.

    You don't have to
    do anything, say anything.
    Seems you just have to be you.

Grown-ups think they know.
Bullies? Just cowards, they say,
unsure of *themselves,*
needing to act big.
But it's hard to believe
when jeering faces
zoom up to yours.

When they're hassling you,
calling you names,
leading the chanting,
the whispering,
urging the others on,
a relentless horde
of nagging, pecking birds.

Then there's the 'in-betweens',
the waiting, the not knowing,
just sure that
sooner or later
it's going to come.
The worst times;
the thinking times.

    Don't ask me the answer.
    I don't know but –
    I'm getting there.

Keep my eyes skinned,
find a crowd to vanish into
before *they* see *me*.
Cornered, I know I can't look them
in the eye – but I've learned
not to look at the floor,
to try and walk tall.

Mostly I've learned
to talk in my head,
tell myself
it's not me, I'm all right –
they're the idiots, the misfits.
Eventually
it begins to sink in.

I'm getting tougher inside.
It's working.
Just don't give in.

Try anything, anything.
But don't *let* them win.

'*Bullied*', Patricia Leighton.

Understanding the poem
- According to the poem, who do bullies pick on?
- What does the poet say is the 'worst' time?
- What is the poet learning to do to avoid being picked on?
- What is she determined not to let happen?

Looking at words
Explain the meaning of these words and phrases as they are used in the poem.

a radar   **b** unsure   **c** jeering
d hassling   **e** relentless   **f** eyes skinned
g walk tall   **h** misfits   **i** sink in

Exploring further
- Explain, in your own words, what 'grown-ups' say about bullies.
- In the fourth verse, what does the poet compare bullies to? Explain why you think this is or isn't a good comparison.
- Why do you think the poet has learned 'not to look at the floor'?
- Why do you think it is important that the poet believes 'it's not me, I'm all right'?

Extra
Why do you think people bully other people?

What advice you would give to someone who was being bullied?

The New Boy

The door swung inward. I stood and breathed
The new-school atmosphere:
The smell of polish and disinfectant,
And the flavour of my own fear.

I followed into the cloakroom; the walls
Rang to the shattering noise
Of boys who barged and boys who banged;
Boys and still more boys!

A boot flew by. Its angry owner
Pursued with force and yell;
Somewhere a man snapped orders; somewhere
There clanged a bell.

And there I hung with my new schoolmates;
They pushing and shoving me; I
Unknown, unwanted, pinned to the wall;
On the verge of ready-to-cry.

Then, from the doorway, a boy called out:
'Hey, you over there! You're new!
Don't just stand there propping the wall up!
I'll look after you!'

I turned; I timidly raised my eyes;
He stood and grinned meanwhile;
And my fear died, and my lips answered
Smile for his smile.

He showed me the basins, the rows of pegs;
He hung my cap at the end;
He led me away to my new classroom …
And now that boy's my friend.

'The New Boy', John Walsh

Understanding the poem

1 What is the setting for the poem?

2 What smells does the poet notice?

3 When the poet was 'pinned to the wall', what was he about to do?

4 When did the poet's 'fear' die?

Understanding the words

5 Explain the meaning of the following words and phrases as they are used in the poem.

  a atmosphere   **b** shattering   **c** pursued

  d on the verge   **e** timidly

Exploring Further

6 Find evidence in the poem that tells you how the boy was feeling at the beginning of the poem.

7 Find evidence that tells you how he was feeling at the end of the poem.

8 What impression is the poet trying to create with the words 'barged', 'banged' and 'pushing and shoving'?

9 Do you think the boys were being deliberately unkind to the poet? Why? Why not?

10 There are 'Boys and still more boys' in the school. Why do you think it took only one boy being kind to the poet to make him feel better?

Extra

Imagine you had to move to a new school. Write about what you would look forward to and what you would be worried about.

Endurance's Last Voyage

After long months of **ceaseless** anxiety and strain, after times when hope beat high
and times when the outlook was black indeed, the end of the *Endurance* has come.
But though we have been **compelled** to abandon the ship, which is crushed beyond all
hope of ever being righted, we are alive and well, and we have stores and equipment
for the task that lies before us. The task is to reach land with all the members of the
Expedition. It is hard to write what I feel. To a sailor his ship is more than a floating
home, and in the Endurance, I had centred ambitions, hopes and desires. Now, straining
and groaning, her timbers cracking and her wounds gaping, she is slowly giving up

her **sentient** life at the very outset of her career. She is crushed and abandoned after drifting more than 570 miles in a north-westerly direction during the 281 days since she became locked in the ice … We are now 346 miles from Paulet Island, the nearest point where there is any possibility of finding food and shelter. A small hut built there by the Swedish expedition in 1902 is filled with stores left by the Argentine relief ship …

This morning, our last on the ship, the weather was clear, with a gentle south-south-easterly to south-south-westerly breeze. From the crow's nest there was no sign of land of any sort. The pressure was increasing steadily, and the passing hours brought no relief or **respite** for the ship. The attack of the ice reached its climax at 4 p.m. The ship was hove stern up by the pressure, and the driving floe, moving **laterally** across the stern, split the rudder and tore out the rudder-post and stern-post. Then, while we watched, the ice loosened and the *Endurance* sank a little. The decks were breaking upwards and the water was pouring in below. Again the pressure began, and at 5 p.m. I ordered all hands on to the ice. The twisting, grinding **floes** were working their will at last on the ship. It was a sickening sensation to feel the decks breaking up under one's feet, the great beams bending and then snapping with a noise like heavy gun-fire …

Just before leaving, I looked down the engine-room skylight as I stood on the quivering deck, and saw the engines dropping sideways as the stays and bed-plates gave way. I cannot describe the impression of relentless destruction that was forced upon me as I looked down and around. The floes, with the force of millions of tons of moving ice behind them, were simply **annihilating** the ship …

South, Sir Ernest Shackleton

› Who is the author of the autobiography?

› What is the name of the ship?

› Where do they have to get to, to find food and shelter?

› At what time did they leave the ship and go on to the ice?

› Explain the meaning of the words in **bold**.

› Find evidence in the extract to show that Shackleton:
  • tried to be positive in this situation
  • was very upset about losing the ship.

› Find an example where Shackleton:
  • records a fact
  • expresses a feeling.

› What impression do you get of Shackleton?

› Do you think the extract gives a good impression of the awful situation Shackleton and his men find themselves in? Explain your reasons.

20 HRS, 40 MIN ...
Our Flight in the Friendship

In 1928, Amelia Earhart was the first woman to cross the Atlantic by aeroplane. Along with Wilmer (Bill) Stultz and Louis ('Slim') Gordon, she flew from Trepassey in Canada to Burry Port in the United Kingdom.

> Can't use radio at all. Coming down now in a rather clear spot. 2500 ft. Everything sliding forward.
> 8:50. 2 Boats!!!!
> Trans steamer.
> Try to get bearing. Radio won't work. One hr's gas. Mess.
> All craft cutting our course. Why?

So the log ends.

Its last page records that we had but one hour's supply of gas left; that the time for reaching Ireland had passed; that the course of the vessel sighted perplexed us; that our radio was useless.

Where were we? Should we keep faith with our course and continue?

'Mess' epitomised the blackness of the moment. Were we beaten?

We all favoured sticking to the course. We had to. With faith lost in that, it was hopeless to carry on. Besides, when last we checked it, before the radio went dead, the plane had been holding true.

We circled the *America*, although having no idea of her identity at the time. With the radio crippled, in an effort to get our position, Bill scribbled a note. The note

Understanding the autobiography

- Where did the flight take off from?
- What was:
    a the intended destination   **b** the actual destination?
- What was the name of the aeroplane?
- How long did the flight take?
- What were the two main problems towards the end of the flight?

Looking at words

Explain the meaning of these words and phrases as they are used in the extract.

a bearing   **b** log   **c** perplexed
d keep faith   **e** epitomised   **f** holding true
g fuselage   **h** altitude   **i** nebulous

and an orange to weight it, I tied in a bag with an absurd piece of silver cord. As we circled the *America*, the bag was dropped through the hatch. But the combination of our speed, the movement of the vessel, the wind and the lightness of the missile was too much for our marksmanship. We tried another shot, using our remaining orange. No luck.

Should we seek safety and try to come down beside the steamer? Perhaps one reason the attempt was never attempted was the roughness of the sea which not only made a landing difficult but a take-off impossible.

Bill leaped to the radio with the hope of at least receiving a message. At some moment in the excitement, before I closed the hatch which opens in the bottom of the fuselage I lay flat and took a photograph. This, I am told, is the first one made of a vessel at sea from a plane in trans-Atlantic flight …

We could see only a few miles of water, which melted into the greyness on all sides. The ceiling was so low we could fly at an altitude of only 500 feet. As we moved, our miniature world of visibility, bounded by its walls of mist, moved with us. Half an hour later into it suddenly swam a fishing vessel. In a matter of minutes a fleet of small craft, probably fishing vessels, were almost below us. Happily their course paralleled ours. Although the gasoline in the tanks was vanishing fast, we began to feel land – some land – must be near. It might not be Ireland, but any land would do just then.

Bill, of course, was at the controls. Slim, gnawing a sandwich, sat beside him, when out of the mists there grew a blue shadow, in appearance no more solid than hundreds of other nebulous 'landscapes' we had sighted before. For a while Slim studied it, then turned and called Bill's attention to it.

It was land!

20HRS, 40 MIN … Our Flight in the Friendship, Amelia Earhart

Exploring further
- What do you think the *America* was?
- When Bill dropped the notes, what was he trying to find out?
- Explain, in your own words, why they had 'no luck' with the notes.
- Reread the paragraph beginning, 'We could see only a few miles of water …' How do you think they were feeling:
  a before they saw the fishing vessel   **b** after they saw the fishing vessel?
- What impression do you get of Amelia Earhart?

Extra
The flight across the Atlantic is 2,246 miles. Look at the photograph of Amelia Earhart and her plane.
- Why do you think she went on such a dangerous journey?
- Would you have done it or not? Explain your reasons.

Touching the Void

In June 1985, Joe Simpson and Simon Yates climbed 21,000 ft to the top of Siula Grande in the Andes. On the way down, disaster struck! Joe's ice hammer came out of the mountain wall and …

… there was a sharp cracking sound and my right hand, gripping the axe, pulled down. The sudden jerk turned me outwards and instantly I was falling.

I hit the slope at the base of the cliff before I saw it coming. I was facing into the slope and both knees locked as I struck it. I felt a shattering blow in my knee, felt bones splitting, and screamed. The impact catapulted me over backwards and down the slope of the East Face. I slid, head-first, on my back. The rushing speed of it confused me. I thought of the drop below but felt nothing. Simon would be ripped off the mountain. He couldn't hold this. I screamed again as I jerked to a sudden violent stop.

Everything was still, silent. My thoughts raced madly. Then pain flooded down my thigh – a fierce burning fire coming down the inside of my thigh, seeming to ball in my groin, building and building until I cried out at it, and my breathing came in ragged gasps. My leg! Oh Jesus. My leg!

I hung, head down, on my back, left leg tangled in the rope above me, and my right leg hanging slackly to one side. I lifted my head from the snow and stared, up across my chest, at a grotesque distortion in the right knee, twisting the leg into a strange zigzag. I didn't connect it with the pain which burnt in my groin. That had nothing to do with my knee. I kicked my left leg free of the rope and swung round until I was hanging against the snow on my chest, feet down. The pain eased. I kicked my left foot into the slope and stood up.

A wave of nausea surged over me. I pressed my face into the snow, and the sharp cold seemed to calm me. Something terrible, something dark with dread occurred to me, and as I thought about it I felt the dark thought break into panic: 'I've broken my leg, that's it. I'm dead. Everyone said it … if there's just two of you a broken ankle could turn into a death sentence … if it's broken … if … It doesn't hurt so much, maybe I've just ripped something.'

I kicked my right leg against the slope, feeling sure it wasn't broken. My knee exploded. Bone grated, and the fireball rushed from groin to knee. I screamed. I looked down at the knee and could see it was broken, yet I tried not to believe what I was seeing. It wasn't just broken, it was ruptured, twisted, crushed, and I could see the kink in the joint and knew what had happened. The impact had driven my lower leg up through the knee joint.

Touching the Void, Joe Simpson

Understanding the autobiography

  1 Name the two men climbing in the Andes.

  2 Which mountain were they climbing?

  3 Which side of the mountain were they on?

  4 What could a minor injury, such a broken ankle, mean for only two climbers on a mountain?

Understanding the words

  5 Explain the meaning of these words and phrases as they are used in the extract.

    a locked   **b** catapulted   **c** grotesque distortion

    d nausea   **e** ruptured   **f** impact

Exploring further

  6 What do you think Joe means when he says, 'Simon would be ripped off the mountain. He couldn't hold this'?

  7 Joe says, 'My thoughts raced madly'. What 'thoughts' do you think were going through his mind at this point?

  8 Explain, in your own words, what the 'something dark with dread' was that occurred to Joe.

  9 Joe's right leg was injured. Why do you think he kicked it 'against the slope'?

10 What impression do you get of Joe Simpson?

Extra

Simon was above Joe on the mountain. He couldn't see what had happened but he knew something was wrong.

Imagine you are Simon and write briefly about the incident from your point of view. Remember that as well as the facts, you need to include your thoughts and feelings.

The Tower of London

History of the Tower of London

William the Conqueror (1035–1087) built the Tower of London for the purpose of protecting the city. **Tradition** has it that it was started in 1078 and took 20 years to complete. The White Tower was the first stone keep to be built in Britain and is the only part left of the original building. Large quantities of stone were **transported** to the site to build the huge walls that extended 33.5 metres east/west, 36.5 metres north/south, and were 27.5 metres high. Over the centuries, the buildings on the site have been extended and now, including the moat, cover 18 acres.

In the reign of Henry III (1216–1272) the Tower was extended and enclosed by a new **curtain wall**. Edward I (1272–1307) continued improving the castle's defences by having two curtain walls, one inside the other. The inner wall was higher so the outer wall could be defended from it.

Throughout its history, the Tower of London has been **fortress**, palace and prison; the home of the Royal Mint and the Royal Observatory; housed a large **arsenal** of small arms and the Crown Jewels. From the 13th century onwards it was also the home of the Royal Menagerie that evolved into London Zoo.

Up until as late as the 17th century, control of the Tower of London was essential to control of London itself. The Tower was a stronghold from which London could be defended, but it was also a **refuge** for when the **monarch** was in danger. Safe within its walls, a monarch could organise his supporters or come to some agreement with the enemy – an enemy that was often the people of London, who were less than pleased with their monarch's actions.

The Tower of London became one of many royal houses. In many reigns it was hardly used at all, but almost every monarch stayed there before his or her **coronation**. After spending the night at the Tower, the monarch-to-be would ride in a great procession through the streets of London to Westminster Abbey to be crowned. This procession was to please the people of London whose support was so important to a successful reign. The last of these processions from the Tower to the Abbey was made by Charles II in 1661.

Although no monarch has actually lived in the Tower of London for over 400 years, it still has the title of a royal palace.

› For what purpose was the Tower of London built?

› How many acres does the site now cover?

› When did 'almost every monarch' stay at the Tower of London?

› Where are the kings and queens of England crowned?

› Explain the meaning of the words and phrases in **bold**.

› What do you understand by the phrase 'Tradition has it'?

› What do you think was the purpose of:
  • the Royal Mint
  • the Royal Observatory?

› Why do you think the monarch had 'to please the people of London'?

› How has the writer organised the information about the Tower of London?

› Do you think the photographs help the reader to understand the text? Why? Why not?

› This is the introduction to a guidebook about the Tower of London. Do you think it is useful or not? Explain your reasons.

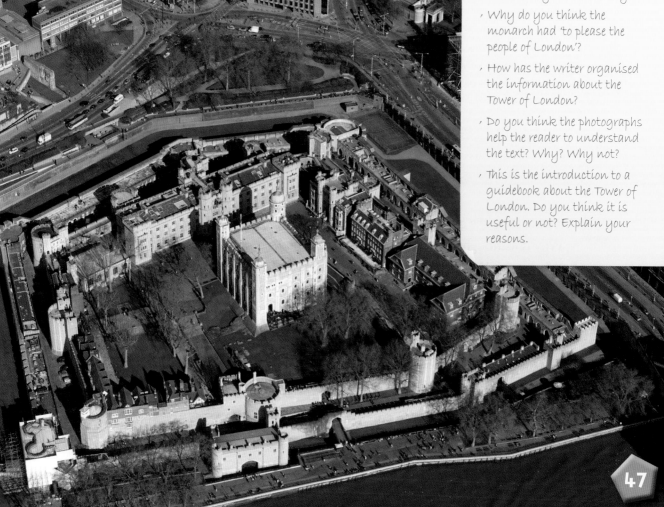

A GUIDE TO

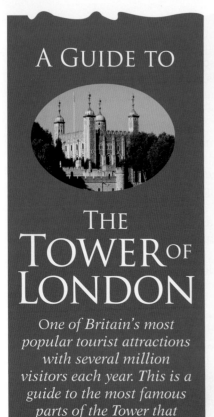

THE
TOWER OF
LONDON

One of Britain's most popular tourist attractions with several million visitors each year. This is a guide to the most famous parts of the Tower that should not be missed.

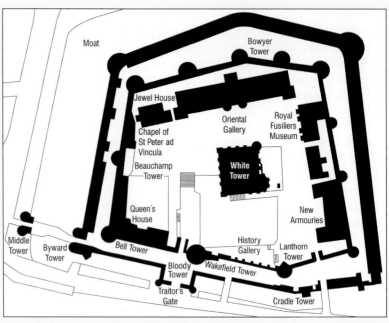

The Armouries

Housed in the White Tower, armour and weapons from the Middle Ages onward are displayed in the Armouries. The earliest examples are of chain mail for the body and legs. A helmet was worn and extra protection given by a shield carried on the left arm. Weapons were the lance and the sword and, to a lesser degree, the mace and the axe. As well as weapons and armour used for sport, tournaments and combat, one can also see an example of an execution block and axe. Oriental weapons are on display in the New Armouries to the east of the White Tower.

Understanding the guide

- Why is it thought the name of the Garden Tower was changed?
- What is the Wakefield Tower most famous for?
- Who wore the Imperial State Crown at her coronation?
- Where were people tried before being imprisoned in the Tower?

Looking at words

Explain the meaning of these words and phrases as they are used in the guide.

a to a lesser degree	**b** mace	**c** combat
d sceptre	**e** orbs	**f** male heir
g treason	**h** Formerly known as	**i** gruesome

Traitor's Gate

Traitor's Gate is situated below St Thomas's Tower. It was originally a main entrance via the Thames. In later years it was used to bring prisoners to the Tower after they had been tried and convicted at Westminster. Such famous prisoners as Anne Boleyn, Sir Thomas More and Thomas Cromwell passed through these gates on the way to imprisonment or execution.

The Jewel House

Most of the jewels on display date from the 17th century as many of the earlier ones were melted down by Oliver Cromwell. The oldest crown to be seen was made for the coronation of Charles II. Other items, such as Queen Victoria's Imperial State Crown, sceptre, orbs and swords, can be seen in the Jewel House.

The Wakefield Tower

Probably named after William de Wakefield, a senior court official in the reign of Edward III, it is most famous for being the scene of Anne Boleyn's trial. The second wife of Henry VIII failed to produce a male heir. Charges of treason were brought against her and she was executed in 1536.

The Bloody Tower

Formerly known as the Garden Tower, it was given its gruesome name because of the deaths of 'the Princes in the Tower'. Edward V (12) and his brother, the Duke of York (10), are thought to have been murdered by the Duke of Gloucester on his way to becoming King Richard III.

Exploring further
- How do you think the writer of the guide worked out which are the 'most popular' parts of the Tower?
- Why do you think the Duke of Gloucester may have murdered the princes?
- Do you think Charles II ruled England before or after Oliver Cromwell? Explain your reasons.
- Why do you think 'Traitor's Gate' is so called?
- Why do you think the writer has included a plan of the Tower of London?

Extra
Using the plan of the Tower, work out a circular route so that a visitor sees everything mentioned in the guide.

Spectres of the Past

During the Tower of London's 900-year history, it has become known as one of the most haunted places in Britain.

The first reported sighting

Thomas Becket was the Archbishop of Canterbury in the reign of Henry II. He quarrelled with the king and was murdered in Canterbury Cathedral on Henry's orders. When Henry III, Henry II's grandson, was building a curtain wall at the Tower of London, the story goes that the ghost of Thomas Becket appeared and struck the wall with his cross, reducing it to rubble. Henry III lost no time in naming a tower after Becket to appease his ghost, which was never seen again.

The princes in the Tower

Tradition says that the princes were locked up in the Bloody Tower and put to death on the orders of the future king, Richard III. In the late 15th century, guards passing the Bloody Tower reported two small figures gliding down the stairs. They wore the nightshirts the princes had on when they disappeared. They stood hand in hand before they seemed to fade back into the wall.

The most persistent haunting

The ghost that appears more than any other is that of Anne Boleyn. Accounts persist that she appears near the Queen's House, close to the site of her execution. Her headless body has also been sighted walking the corridors of the Tower.

A gruesome execution

The Countess of Salisbury was put to death by order of King Henry VIII. She would not put

her head on the block and ran from her executioner. He pursued her, attacking her with the axe until she was dead. Some say they have seen her ghost re-enacting her death and the shadow of the axe hanging over the scene of her murder.

The Salt Tower

This is one of the most haunted areas of the Tower of London. Some say dogs will not enter the Salt Tower since a guard was nearly strangled by 'an unseen force'. In 1864 a soldier guarding the Queen's House challenged what he thought was an intruder. Getting no reply he charged with his bayonet and went straight through the apparition.

Understanding the guide

1 How old is the Tower of London?
2 Who saw the ghosts of the two princes?
3 Which ghost appears more than any other?
4 Which is the most haunted area of the Tower?

Understanding the words

5 Explain the meaning of these words and phrases as they are used in the guide.

a the story goes   b appease   c future king   d persist
e pursued   f re-enacting   g bayonet   h apparition

Exploring further

6 What evidence is there in the guide to show that Henry III probably believed in ghosts?
7 What do you understand about the story of the princes in the Tower from the phrase 'Tradition says'?
8 Why do you think the ghost of Anne Boleyn appears 'headless'?
9 What do most of these ghosts have in common?
10 Why do you think the writer has included these ghost stories in the guide?

Extra

Has the guide to the Tower of London made you want to visit it or not? Explain your reasons.

Why the Whales Came

'As long as we keep Scilly Rock **astern** of us we can pull home easily enough,' Daniel said softly.

'But how are we going to do that if we can't see it?' I whispered, taking the oar he was handing me. 'I can't see it anymore.'

'We can hear it though, can't we?' he said. 'Listen.' And certainly I could hear the surge of the sea **seething** around Scilly Rock as it always did even on the calmest of days. 'Hear it?' he said. 'Just keep that sound astern of us and we'll be able to feel our way home. Gweal must be dead ahead from here. There's no **swell** to speak of, so we won't go on the rocks. All we have to do is **to hug the coast** all the way round and that'll bring us nicely into Popplestones.'

And so we began to row, only a few strokes at a time, stopping to listen for the sea around Scilly Rock. It was not long though before I began to think that Gweal was not at all where it should have been. We had already been rowing quite long enough and hard enough to have reached it by now. Then I thought that, perhaps the current must have dragged us off course, that we must be somewhere between Samson and Bryher, that I could still hear Scilly Rock somewhere astern of us and distant, but Daniel was no longer even sure of that. We pulled until our arms could pull no longer, but still no land **loomed** up out of the fog as we expected. Within half an hour we had to admit to each other that we were quite lost. We sat over our oars and drifted, straining our ears for the wash of the sea against the rocks, anything to give us some idea of where we were. The fog though seemed to **obscure** and shroud the sounds of the sea just as it was hiding the islands that we knew lay all around us. Even the piping of invisible oystercatchers was dulled and deadened as the dark came down through the fog and settled around us.

Strange as it may seem, the darkness came as a kind of comfort to us, for at least it was the kind of blindness we were accustomed to. Even Daniel who was never fond of the dark seemed relieved at the **onset** of night. We searched now for some crack in the blackness about us, a glimmer of a light from the shore that would guide us safely home. We sat beside each other huddled together and silent, the damp jibsail wrapped around us to keep out the cold, peering constantly into the **impenetrable** night and listening, always listening for the hiss of surf on the shingle or the distant **muted** charge of the waves against the cliffs.

Often during that long, long night our hopes were raised by the whisper

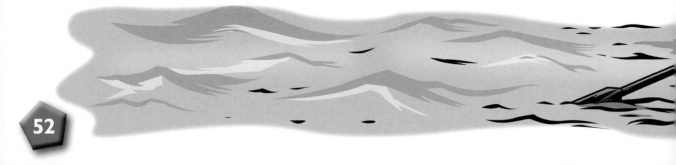

of waves on some far shore, and we would row frantically towards it for a few minutes and then sit silent and listen again, only to discover it had been nothing but wishful thinking, a trick of the mind. Either it was that or we had simply been rowing the wrong way – we could never be sure which. In this dense darkness all sense of direction, time and space seemed to be **distorted**. Each time our hopes were raised only to be dashed, and each time the disappointment was all the more cruel and all the more lasting.

The cold had numbed my feet up to my knees and my hands could no longer feel the oar I was pulling. I wanted so much just to go to sleep, to give up and go to sleep. But Daniel would not let me.

Why the Whales Came, Michael Morpurgo

> › What is the setting for this part of the story?
>
> › At the beginning of the extract, why can't the characters see Scilly Rock?
>
> › What does Daniel say they can use to find their way home?
>
> › How is the narrator feeling at the end of the extract?
>
> › Explain the meaning of the words and phrases in **bold**.
>
> › Explain, in your own words, why the narrator says, 'the darkness came as a kind of comfort to us'.
>
> › What does the narrator mean when she says that 'the whisper of waves on some far shore' was only 'wishful thinking'?
>
> › Why do you think Daniel would not let the narrator go to sleep?
>
> › When you read this extract, how does the writer want you to feel?

53

Lost at Sea

Jessie Parsons lives on Clare Island. Her American cousin, Jack, comes to stay with her for the summer. Jessie's father takes them fishing but has to return home when his rod breaks, leaving the children on the rocks. Then disaster strikes!

That was the moment the fish caught on and Jack shouted, 'I've got one! I've got one!' He braced his legs and began to reel in furiously. Then he slipped. His legs went from under him and he was sliding past her towards the edge.

Instinctively, Jessie reached out for him. For a fleeting moment she had hold of his jeans, just long enough for Jack to cling on to a rock and stop his slide. But then Jessie herself was slipping, rolling over and over and over, trying to find something to clutch at, anything. But there was nothing, no way she could stop herself. She caught a glimpse of Jack throwing himself full-stretch on the rock to save her. Then she was over the edge and falling through the air. The sea smothered her before she could scream. The water came into her mouth and into her ears and she was sinking deeper and deeper and could do nothing about it.

She looked up. There was light up above her, light she knew she had to reach if she was to live, but her legs wouldn't kick and her flailing arms seemed incapable of helping her. She had often thought about how drowning would be, when she was out in her father's boat or crossing over from the mainland on the ferry. And now she was drowning. This was how it was. Her eyes were stinging, so she closed them. She closed her mouth too, so she wouldn't swallow any more seawater. But she had to breathe – she couldn't help herself. She gasped and the seawater came in again and she began to choke.

Understanding the extract

- What are the two settings for this extract?
- What caused Jack to slip?
- What was Jessie trying to do when she slipped?
- What happened before she could scream?
- What did Jack say they had to keep doing?

Looking at words
Explain the meaning of these words and phrases as they are used in the extract.

a furiously   **b** Instinctively   **c** fleeting moment
d flailing   **e** shrouded   **f** whimper

Then something was holding her down. She fought, but the grip tightened about her waist and would not let go. Her head broke water, and suddenly there was air, wonderful air to breathe. She was spluttering and coughing. Someone was shouting at her. It was Jack and he was holding her. 'It's me! It's me! Hang on, just hang on to me. You'll be OK.' His face was near hers. 'Can you swim?' She shook her head. 'Just try to keep your mouth closed. Someone'll see us. We'll be OK. We'll be fine.'

Jessie looked beyond him. The shore was already a long way off and they were being carried away from it all the time. She looked the other way. Whenever they came up to the top of a wave she could see the bank of mist rolling over the sea towards them. One more wave and the mist would swallow them and then no one would ever see them.

'We've got to keep floating,' Jack cried. 'Just hang on.' The cold had numbed her legs already and she knew her arms couldn't hold on much longer. And then the mist came over their heads and shrouded them completely. Jack was crying out for help, screaming. She tried herself, but could only manage a whimper. It was hopeless.

The Ghost of Grania O'Malley, Michael Morpurgo

Exploring further
- What do you think was going through Jessie's mind as she was falling?
- Why do you think she 'fought' when Jack was trying to rescue her?
- Do you think Jack believed what he was saying when he said, 'We'll be fine'? Explain your reasons.
- Explain, in your own words, why Jessie did not believe him.
- How do you think Jack felt when:
    a he saw Jessie going into the water
    b he dived in to save her
    c he was 'crying out for help'?

Extra
What do you think Jack and Jessie can do to save themselves?

Alone in the Ocean

Michael's parents are both made redundant. His father decides to buy a boat called the Peggy Sue. So Michael, his mum and dad, and their dog Stella, set off to sail round the world. One night his parents are sleeping and Michael is in charge of the boat. Stella is barking and she hasn't got her safety harness on …

… So I left the wheel and went forward to bring her back. I took the ball with me to sweeten her in, to tempt her away from the bow of the boat.

I crouched down. 'Come on, Stella,' I said, rolling the ball from hand to hand. 'Come and get the ball.' I felt the boat turn a little in the wind, and I knew then I shouldn't have left the wheel. The ball rolled away from me quite suddenly. I lunged after it, but it was gone over the side before I could grab it. I lay there on the deck watching it bob away into the darkness. I was furious with myself for being so silly.

I was still cursing myself when I thought I heard the sound of singing. Someone was singing out there in the darkness. I called but no one replied. So that was what Stella had been barking at.

I looked again for my ball, but by now it had disappeared. That ball had been very precious to me, precious to all of us. I knew I had just lost a great deal more than a football.

I was angry with Stella. The whole thing had been her fault. She was still barking. I couldn't hear the singing anymore. I called her again, whistled her in. She wouldn't come. I got to my feet and went forward. I took her by the collar and pulled. She would not be moved. I couldn't drag her all the way back, so I bent down to pick her up. She was still reluctant. Then I had her in my arms, but she was struggling.

I heard the wind above me in the sail. I remember thinking: this is silly, you haven't got your safety harness on, you haven't got your lifejacket on, you shouldn't be doing this. Then the boat veered violently and I was thrown sideways. With my arms full I had no time to grab the guard rail. We were in the cold of the sea before I could even open my mouth to scream.

The terrors came fast, one upon another. The lights of the Peggy Sue went away in the dark of the night, leaving me alone in the ocean, alone with the certainty that they were already too far away, that my cries for help could not possibly be heard. I thought then of sharks cruising the black water beneath me – scenting me, already searching me out, homing in on me – and I knew there could be no hope. I would be eaten alive. Either that or I would drown slowly. Nothing could save me.

Kensuke's Kingdom, Michael Morpurgo

Understanding the extract

1 What is the setting for the extract?
2 Why did Michael think Stella was barking?
3 Why did he pick up the dog?
4 Why did he think he was being 'silly'?
5 What two things frightened Michael when he was in the water?

Understanding the words

6 Explain the meaning of these words and phrases as they are used in the extract.

   a made redundant   **b** sweeten her   **c** lunged
   d still reluctant   **e** veered   **f** cruising

Exploring further

7 Explain in your own words why Michael 'shouldn't have left the wheel'.
8 Why do you think the ball was very 'precious' to him?
9 How do you think Michael felt when he was plunged into 'the cold of the sea'?
10 How do you think Michael gets to safety?

Extra

Write a brief conversation between Michael's parents when they realise he is missing.

The Daily

Late Edition

11th Fe

Devilish Doings in Devon

By Henry Harris

This winter has been the coldest anyone can remember and, two nights ago, the night of the 9th February, was **no exception**. Many parts of the country experienced a heavy snowfall, including Devon where the River Exe froze over, trapping birds in the ice.

The people of Totnes and Littlehampton, however, had more to talk about than the weather when they awoke yesterday morning. Something very **bizarre** had happened – something that no one can quite explain.

The countryside was smooth and white from the overnight snowfall. As would be expected, there were prints from birds and animals here and there. What was not expected was a trail of tracks, seemingly made by a creature with hooves walking on two legs, which stretched for miles across the countryside.

The strange tracks began in a garden in Totnes and covered about 100 miles before simply coming to an end in a field near Littlehampton. What could the explanation be? Many villagers in these parts are in no doubt. The cloven-hooved tracks are the devil's work!

Police were on the scene very quickly and began by investigating the tracks that led into a wood near Dawlish. Dogs were brought to **flush out** the wood but they refused

Police on the trail of a mysterious creature.

to go in, standing at the edge howling pitifully. Proof, say those who support the devil **theory**, that something very mysterious is **afoot**

When asked for his opinion, the leading **naturalist** Sir Richard Owen suggested that a badger had made the tracks. As it normally moves by placing its hind legs in the marks left by its forelegs, this explains why the creature appeared

News

ry 1855

to be two-footed. Mr Sam Coombe, a local farmer, said, 'That may explain the two feet, but it doesn't explain the hooves. I've never seen a badger with hooves'.

Some 'explanations' are truly weird! An **amateur** naturalist suggests that the tracks are those of a kangaroo. When this reporter asked him where the kangaroo could have come from he replied, 'It probably escaped from a travelling zoo and then returned to its cage without anyone noticing'.

Mrs Ruth Standish, a local schoolteacher, **dismisses** the whole thing as a **hoax**, saying that she wouldn't put it past some of the young people in the area to have thought up and **executed** the whole thing as a huge joke.

There are those in the area who are convinced that the tracks were made by a wild beast and have gone, armed with pitchforks, to hunt it down.

Others, however, feel there is a more 'supernatural' explanation. They are bolting their doors and refusing to **venture** outside after sunset. They are playing safe and, until a **rational** explanation is found, believe that on 9th February 1855, the devil walked in Devon.

Villagers find strange tracks in the snow.

- When and where did the incident occur?
- What had happened?
- List the possible explanations given in the article.
- Explain the meaning of the words and phrases in **bold**.
- Why do you think the reporter writes about 'when' and 'where' the incident occurred before writing about the incident itself?
- The dogs would not go into the wood. Why do you think some people saw that as 'proof' of the 'devil theory'?
- Why do you think people wanted Sir Richard Owen's opinion?
- What impression do you get of Mrs Ruth Standish?
- Give examples from the report of a fact and an opinion.
- Do any of the explanations convince you? Why? Why not?

ISLANDS OF Fire

Tongatapu, in the Pacific Ocean to the west of Australia, lies in the island group known as Tonga. On Monday 16 March 2009, about seven miles from Tongatapu, an underwater volcano began erupting. By Wednesday 18 March, so much lava had been ejected that it had formed a new island. On Thursday 19 March, a huge earthquake measuring 7.9 on the Richter scale occurred.

Fear of imminent danger to the surrounding islands prompted the Tsunami Warning Centre to issue a serious alert. Luckily, no damage or loss of life was reported.

The new island is made from pumice that is formed when lava cools rapidly. It is very light and can float. Experts agree that the island will last several months or possibly a few years but, in time, it will be eroded by the sea. A spokesman for the team of scientists on their way to the new island said that they were going to observe the eruption and, when things had quietened down, measure the island.

As well as volcanic eruptions creating islands, they can also make islands virtually disappear. One of the most famous examples is Krakatoa off the southwest coast of Indonesia.

In 1883, Krakatoa covered an area of 23 square kilometres to a height of 450 metres above sea level. On 20 May, there were reports of a plume of smoke rising 10 kilometres above the island. Minor eruptions continued from May to August,

and on 27 August 1883, a series of huge volcanic eruptions occurred, resulting in most of the island being submerged 250 metres below sea level.

Reports at the time say that the final explosion was heard 4,500 kilometres away and caused 40-metre high tsunamis that completely submerged many small islands. The major islands of Java and Sumatra were devastated: whole towns and villages were destroyed and nearly all vegetation was stripped away.

Shipping suffered a similar fate, most being destroyed in the enormous waves. The Berouw, a steamship in the area, was carried 10 metres above sea level and deposited a mile inland.

It has been estimated that over 36,000 people lost their lives, either from the volcanic eruption that rained down ash and produced lava flows that reached up to 700 °C, or from the ensuing tsunamis. As far away as the east coast of Africa, rafts of pumice were washed up, sometimes with a grizzly cargo of human remains.

And Krakatoa has not finished yet. On 29 December 1927 more eruptions took place and a new volcano emerged from the sea, Anak Krakatoa – Child of Krakatoa – which is rumbling to this day, seemingly readying itself for another earth-shattering eruption.

▲ Perboewatan
Anak Krakatau
Island before
26 August 1883
Danan
▲ Rakata
Krakatau Island
0   3 km

Krakatoa as it was before ... and after the explosion.

An eruption of Anak Krakatoa.

Understanding the article
- The article reports three incidents. When and where does each take place?
- In what way are the first and second incidents:
  a similar   **b** different?
- Why are the team of scientists going to the new island?
- What caused the loss of life after the eruption of Krakatoa?

Looking at words
Explain the meaning of these words and phrases as they are used in
the article.

a ejected   **b** Richter scale   **c** imminent   **d** eroded
e virtually   **f** submerged   **g** tsunamis   **h** ensuing

Exploring further
- In addition to the text, how has the writer helped the reader to understand
  the article?
- Give an example of a fact and an opinion.
- Why do you think the writer gives exact dates and measurements
  in the article?
- Why do you think that the number of people who died is only estimated?
- Make a list of questions you would like to ask about Krakatoa.

Extra
Plan an article about an imaginary island with a volcano that erupts. Make
notes on:
- what facts you need
- whose opinion you would include
- how you would illustrate the article
- how you would lay out the article.

*Krakatoa as it was
before the explosion.*

The Northern Lights Fantastic

by Penny Stretton

The Northern Lights sweep startling colours across the frozen night sky as the moon rises over the snow.

A shock of yellow lights up the mountains in Yukon, Canada, threatening to outshine the full moon.

In the nearby Brooks Range, a glow of turquoise and pink bathe an igloo in unearthly light.

And waves of green dance around a streak of white and pink high above an Eskimo monument, or inukshuk, in Hudson Bay, Manitoba.

Photographer Rolf Hicker has spent the last 10 years travelling thousands of miles with his wife Michelle to capture these amazing images.

The Aurora Borealis is only visible at night, and is best seen in winter. It is extremely difficult to capture the full glory of the Northern Lights, especially with a full moon – and most photographers

A rare image of the Northern Lights with a full moon.

An Eskimo inukshuk is illuminated by waves of green dancing lights.

don't bother. But Mr Hicker found a way. He said, 'It's the perfect time to show the Northern Lights with the landscape. If conditions are right, especially when it is very cold, you can experience one of the most amazing moments we ever have – a moonrise with the Aurora Borealis, all at the same time.'

He added: 'The reward for all the trouble is amazing – silence and dancing Northern Lights in the moonlight.'

An igloo looks startlingly white lit up by a flash of turquoise and pink.

Understanding the article

1 Name the three places the photographer has visited to photograph the Northern Lights.

2 What is the other name for the Northern Lights?

3 How many years have Mr Hicker and his wife been travelling to 'capture these amazing images'?

4 What are the best conditions to see the Northern Lights?

Understanding the words

5 Explain the meaning of these words as they are used in the article.

a startling	**b** threatening	**c** outshine
d bathe	**e** unearthly	**f** visible

Exploring further

6 Why do you think the Northern Lights are 'best seen in winter'?

7 What impression do you get of Rolf Hicker?

8 Why do you think most photographers 'don't bother' to try to photograph the Northern Lights?

9 Would the article be as interesting without the photographs? Why? Why not?

10 Explain how you think Rolf Hicker feels when he is watching the Northern Lights. How would you feel?

Extra

Imagine you could interview Rolf Hicker about his travels and photography. What questions would you like to ask him?

How to use this book

This Pupil Book consists of ten units that help to teach comprehension skills for a range of different text types and genres, including fiction, non-fiction and poetry. It can be used on its own or as part of the whole Nelson Comprehension series, including Teacher's Resource Books and CD-ROMs. Each Nelson Comprehension unit is split into three sections.

Teach

The *Teach* section includes an illustrated text for a teacher and children to read together and discuss in class. To help guide the discussion, a series of panel prompt questions is supplied, which can be used to help model a full range of comprehension skills (such as literal understanding, inference and evaluation). Full answer guidance is supplied in the accompanying *Teacher's Resource Book*, with full multi-modal whiteboard support (complete with voiceovers and a range of audio and visual features) on the CD-ROM.

Talk

The aim of this section is to get the children in small groups to practise the skills they have just learnt. Each child could take on a role within the group, such as scribe, reader or advocate. They are presented with a range of questions to practise the skills they have been learning in the *Teach* section.

The questions are followed up by a discussion, drama, role play or other group activity to further reinforce their learning. Further guidance is supplied in the *Teacher's Resource Book*, while interactive group activities to support some of the *Talk* questions and activities are supplied on the CD-ROM.

Write

The third section offers an opportunity to test what the children have learnt by providing a new text extract and a series of questions, which can be answered orally, as a class exercise, or as an individual written exercise. The questions are colour coded according to their type, with initial literal questions, followed by vocabulary clarification, inference and evaluation questions and then an extended follow-up activity. Full answer guidance is supplied in the accompanying *Teacher's Resource Book*, while a whiteboard questioning reviewing feature is supplied on the CD-ROM.